For Lex, Ginger, Bonny and everlasting George.

Published in 2019 by Melbournestyle Books

Melbournestyle Books
155 Clarendon Street, South Melbourne
Victoria 3205, Australia
www.melbournestyle.com.au

 A catalogue record for this book is available from
the National Library of Australia
National Library of Australia Cataloguing-in-Publication entry:

Creator: Coote, Maree, author/illustrator.

Animology: The big book of Letter Art Alphabeasts /
    Maree Coote author, illustrator.

ISBN 978-0-9924917-9-6   (hbk.)

Subjects:
1. Animals -- Pictorial works -- Juvenile literature.
2. Graphic design (Typography) -- Juvenile literature.
3. Alphabet in art -- Pictorial works -- Juvenile literature.
4. Visual poetry, Australian -- Pictorial works -- Juvenile literature.
5. Picture puzzles -- Juvenile literature.

Dewey Number: 421.1

Printed in China by C&C Offset Printing Limited, Co. on wood-free paper

10 9 8 7 6 5 4 3 2 1

Maree Coote's ingenious Letter Art has been awarded the following prizes:
Italy: Bologna Ragazzi Fiere Non-Fiction Special Mention Prize 2017 (Spellbound)
South Korea: Nami Concours Distinction 2017 (Alphabet City Zoo)
USA: Silver Best Illustration Moonbeam Awards 2018 (Letters From New York)
Australia: Shortlisted in CBCA Edith Pownall Award 2018 (Spellbound)

MELBOURNESTYLE
AUSTRALIA

www.melbournestyle.com.au   www.cleverkids.net.au

ANIMOLOGY

LOOK-AND-FIND · EVERY PICTURE MADE WITH THE LETTERS OF ITS OWN NAME · LETTER ART

Every part of me's a letter! Does that help you see me better? Look very closely – can you see The hidden letters that spell me?

Sometimes letters may repeat To make more eyes or fur or feet, Look back-to-front, Look upside-down, Every letter can be found!

MAREE COOTE

These four letters make a frog,
Seen here, jumping from a log.
Lime-green, slime-green, sticky hands
Will help it stay right where it lands.

Can you find these letters that make the picture?

frog

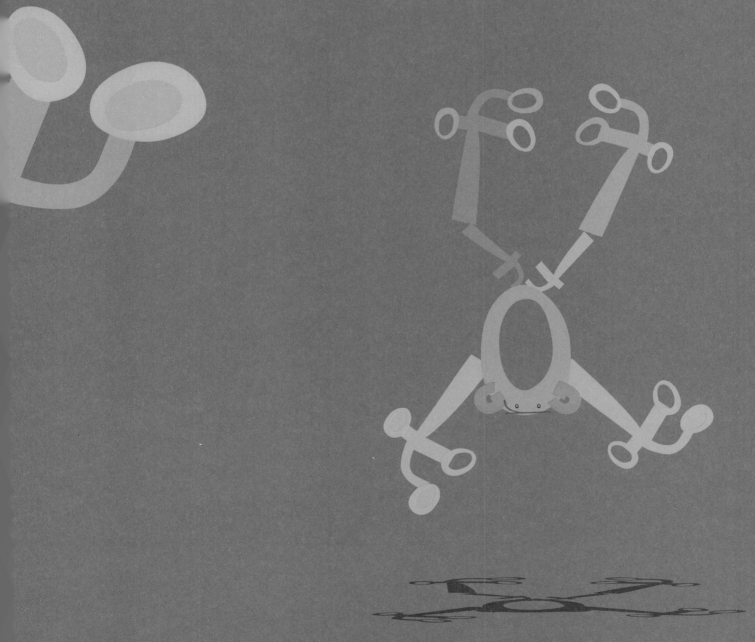

These lovely letters bulge and swish
Until they make a jellyfish,
And then they make a dozen more
To fill the sea and me with awe.

Can you find these letters that make the picture?

jellyfish

Dreaming, lakeside, there was I,
When letters – four – came gliding by.
They spelled themselves into a swan,
And then, serenely, glided on.

Can you find these letters that make the picture?

It isn't that I hate the bath,
It's really just the aftermath:
Despite conditioner, there'll be yelling
When we comb this tangled spelling.

Can you find these letters in the picture?

I stroll about on luscious lawns,
And snack all day on cocktail prawns.
The more I eat, the pinker I'm spelled,
Because I eat my shrimp unshelled.

Can you find these letters in the picture?

fLAMINGO

It's a jungle where I live,
And always so competitive.
To give myself a fighting chance,
I spell danger, in striped pants.

Can you find these letters that make the picture?

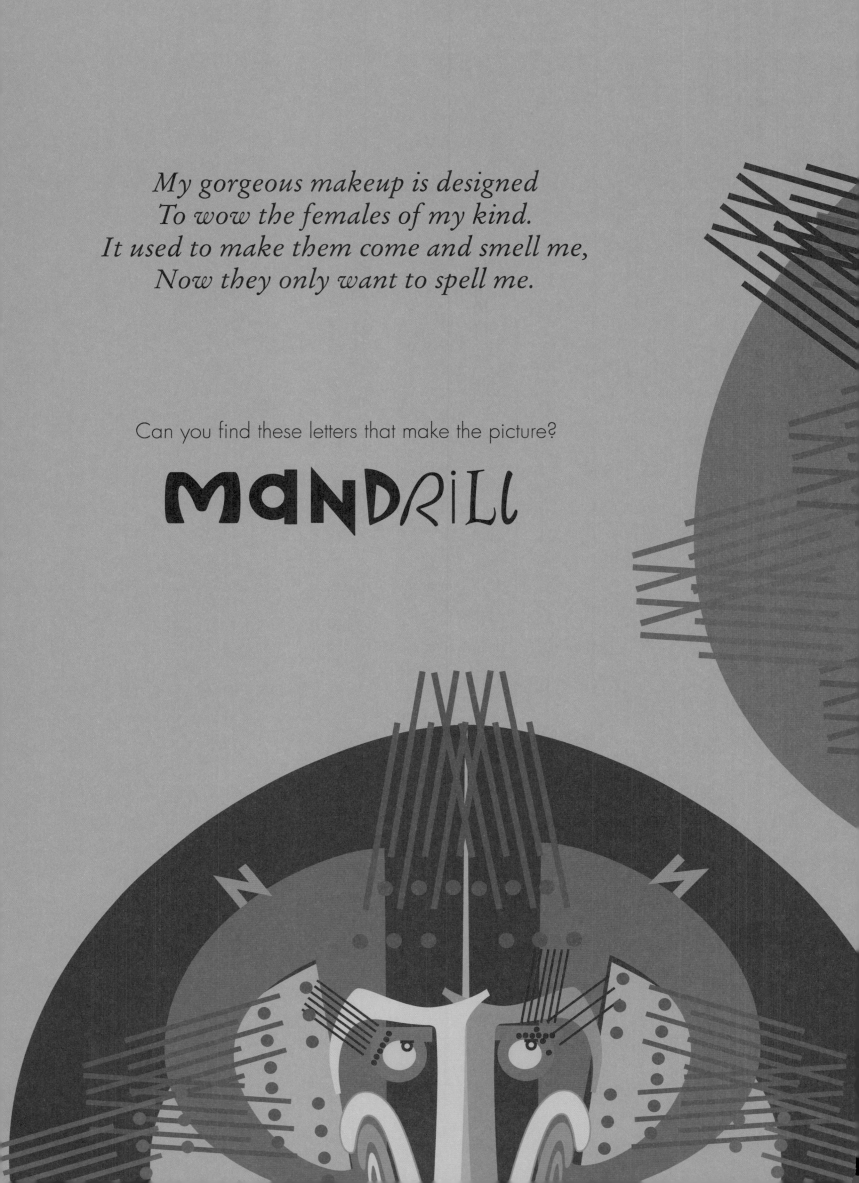

My gorgeous makeup is designed
To wow the females of my kind.
It used to make them come and smell me,
Now they only want to spell me.

Can you find these letters that make the picture?

MANDRILL

My letters spell the fastest bird,
(I've run so fast, my letters blurred!)
I'm hard to match – it's hard to beat me,
If I'm hard to catch – it's hard to eat me.

Can you find these letters that make the picture?

ostrich

Remember when you look at me,
Our ancestors were family.
We share most of our DNA,
The rest of me's just spelled this way.

Can you find these letters that make the picture?

Can you find these letters in the picture?

PEACOCK

Every letter's firmly stuck
In place, so do not try to pluck
One from my splendid multitude
To souvenir a plume – it's rude.

Today, I don't look smart or clever,
But I won't look like this forever –
For two weeks I'll stay spelled this way,
Then pack... and butterfly away!

Can you find these letters that make the picture?

caterpillar

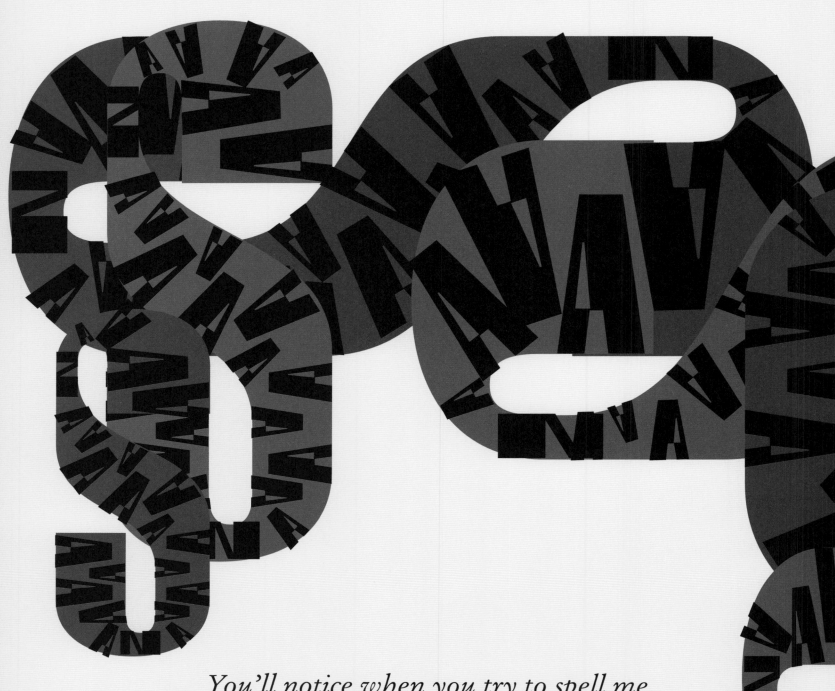

You'll notice when you try to spell me,
Sometimes what I eat can swell me.
I'll show you how — come closer please,
And let me give you a big squeeze.

Can you find these letters in the picture?

SNAKe

When I'm scared I form a ball,
And wait 'til things improve, that's all.
But I'm the same inside, unchanged.
It's just my letters, rearranged.

Can you find these letters in the picture?

ArMADillo

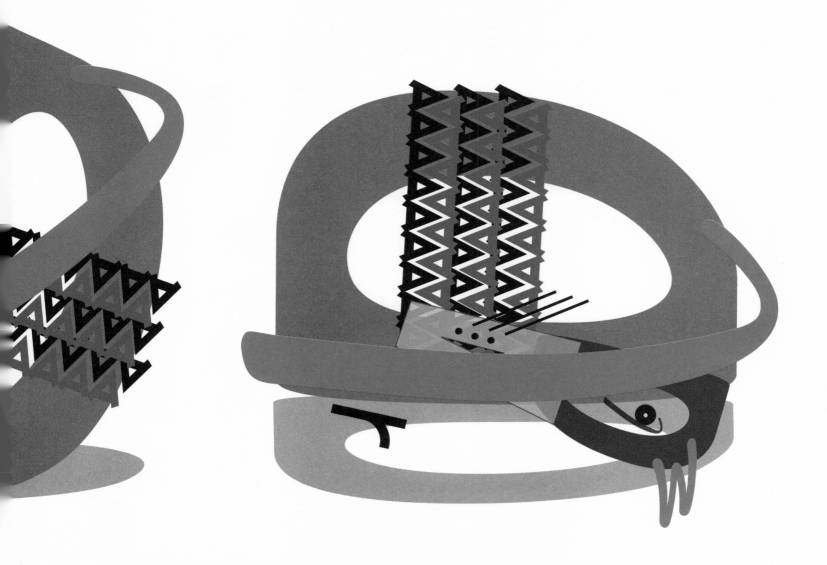

I've got the brains, I don't mind telling,
But, I'm not inclined to teach you spelling.
So ask somebody else to help,
While I spell trouble in the kelp.

Can you find these letters in the picture?

OCTOPUS

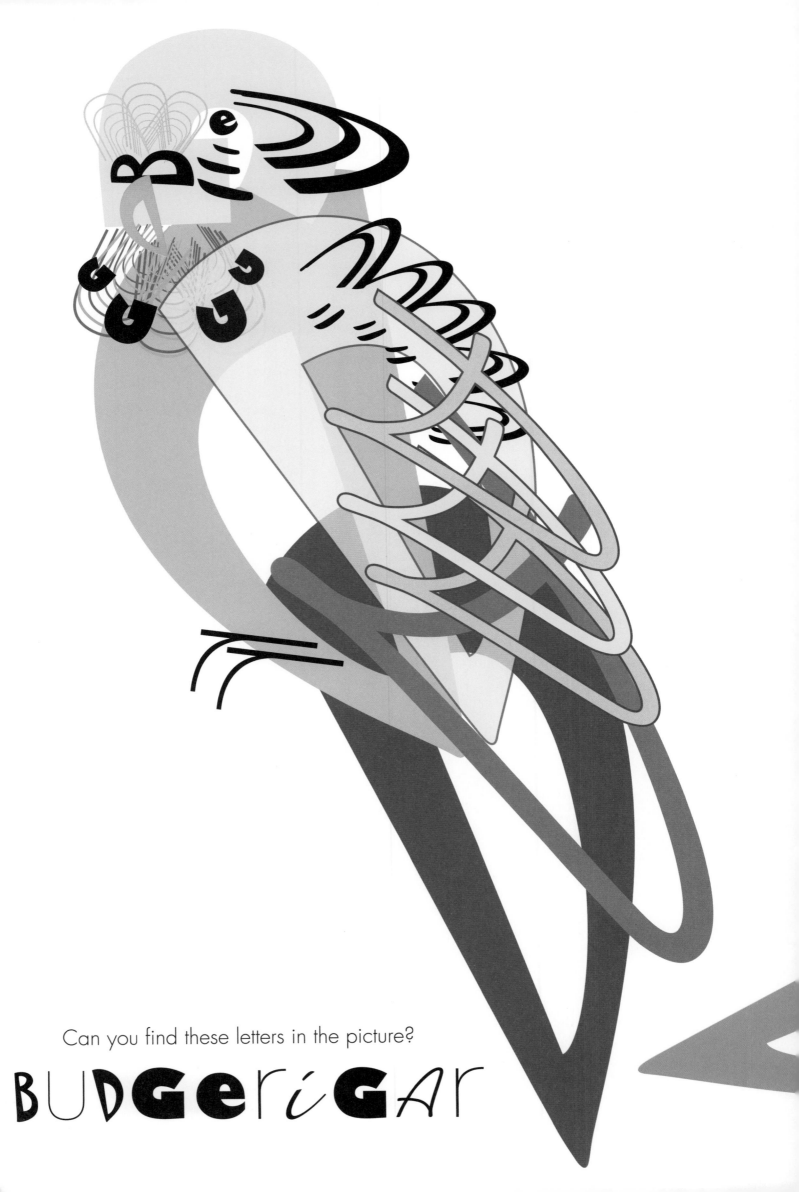

Can you find these letters in the picture?

BUDGeriGAr

These letters, when arranged like this,
Transform by metamorphosis,
Into a pair of talking birds,
Who simply won't stop squawking words.

To get to school, I spell a whale,
And ride inside, down near the tail,
When we arrive, he doesn't stop,
He simply shoots me out the top.

Can you find these letters in the picture?

A special horse, the prancing stallion,
Bred by British and Italian.
They say that quality's genetic,
But clearly, it's all alphabetic.

Can you find these letters in the picture?

STALLion

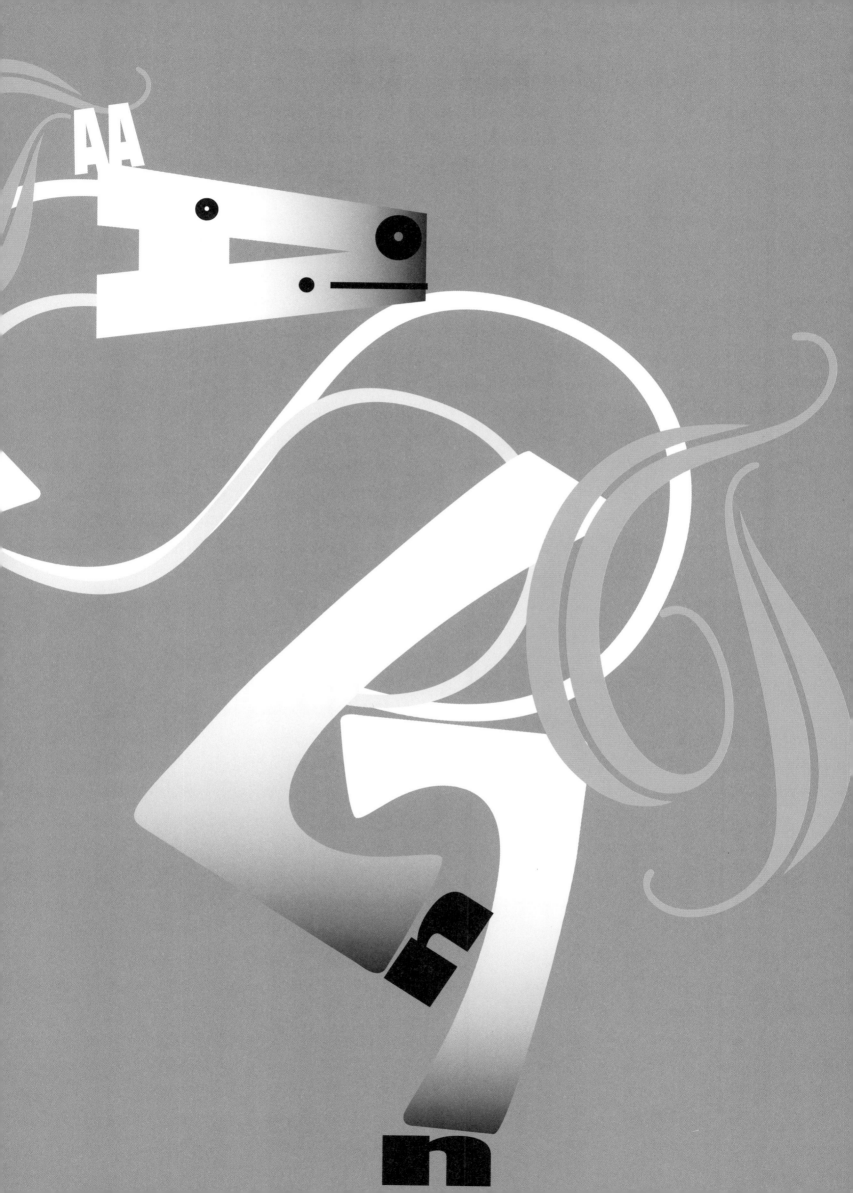

Can you find these letters that make this picture?

CRAb

Don't rush me if I'm running late,
Don't mock me for my wonky gait,
With so few letters used to make me,
Sideways only will they take me.

All the bugs on earth combined,
Completely outweigh humankind.
They had to count them all to tell,
But I think one's enough to spell.

bee TLe

Can you find these letters in the picture?

When we go shopping late at night,
If I get lost, Nan gets a fright.
She gets quite cross if I upset her,
So I keep track of every letter.

Can you find these letters in the picture?

OWL

I don't get up until twelve-thirty,
Don't like getting my paws dirty.
Why get my spelling in a mess
And jeopardize my gorgeousness?

Can you find these letters in the picture?

Afghan hOUnD

Can you find these letters in the picture?

SQUID

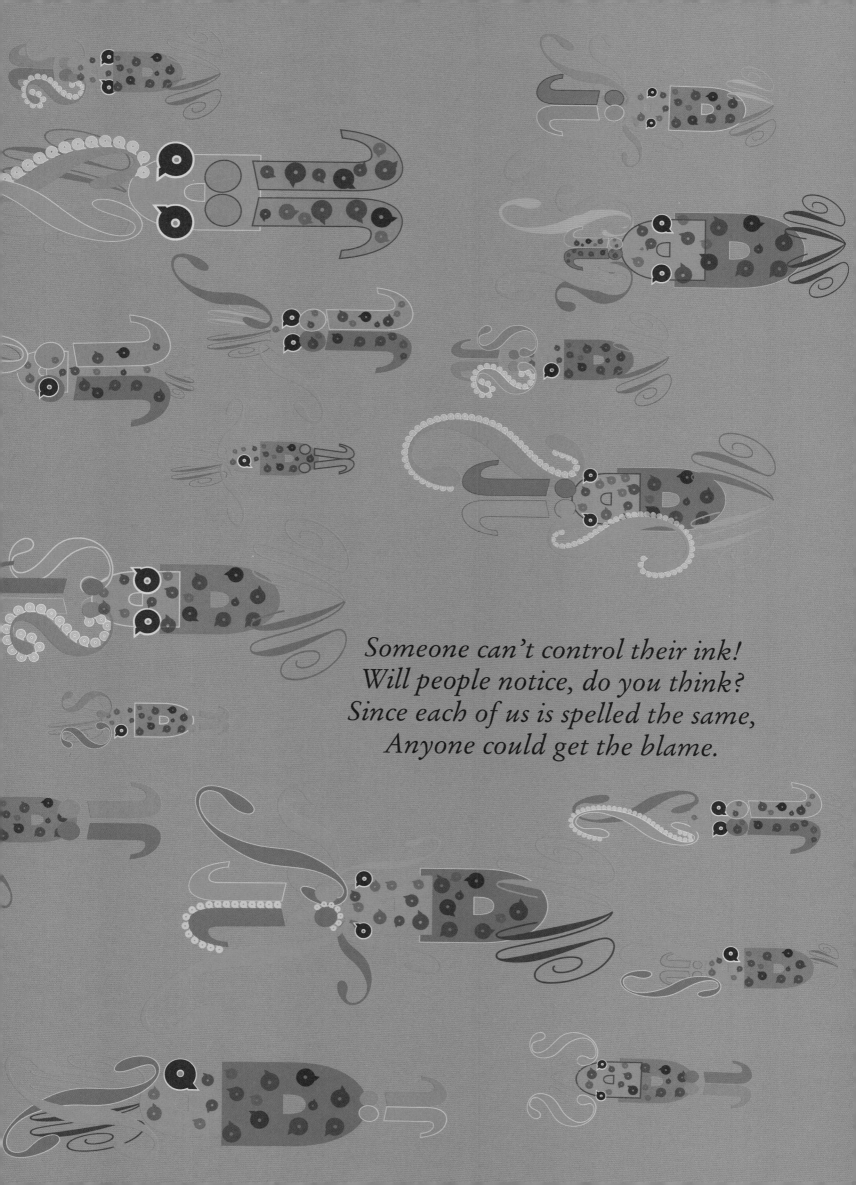

Someone can't control their ink!
Will people notice, do you think?
Since each of us is spelled the same,
Anyone could get the blame.

Can you find these letters that make the picture?

ChAMeleon

The hues of a chameleon
Depend on what she's kneeling on.
The plan is: Camouflage each letter
To hide from letter-hunters better.

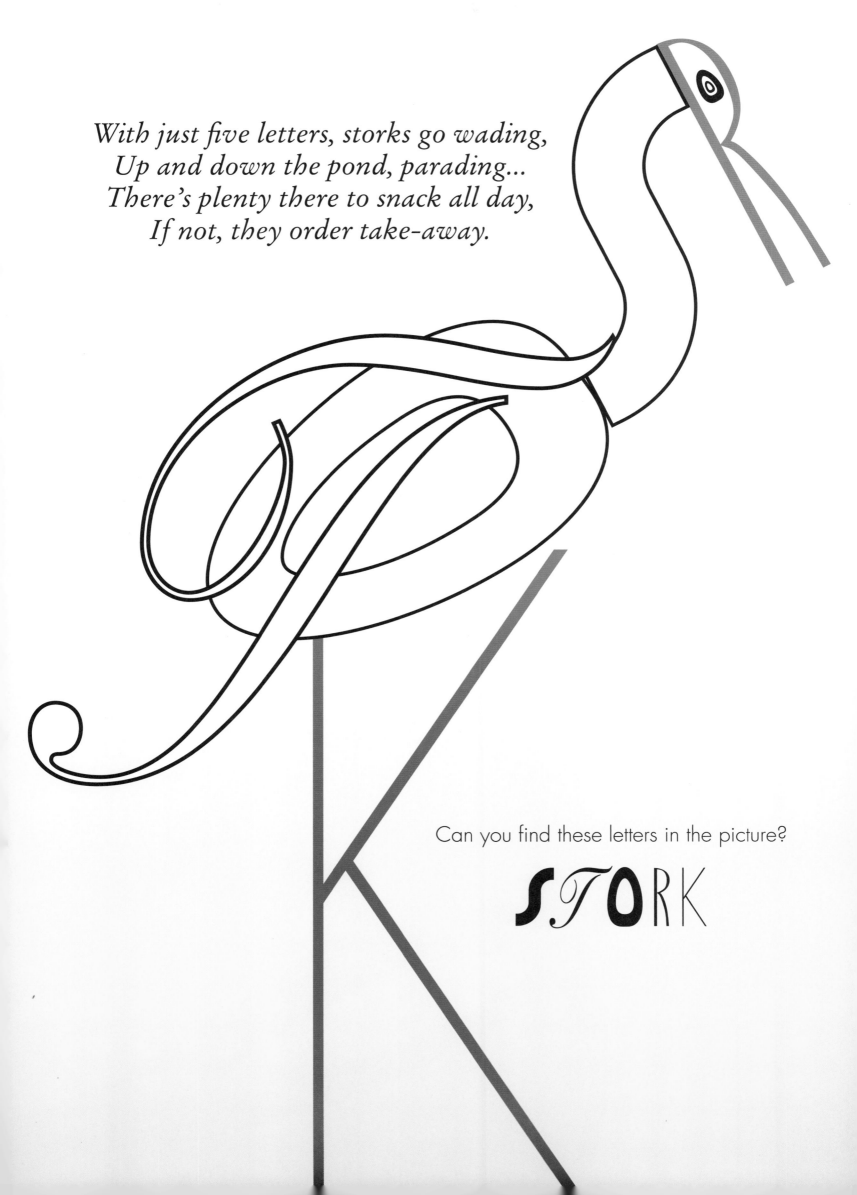

With just five letters, storks go wading,
Up and down the pond, parading...
There's plenty there to snack all day,
If not, they order take-away.

Can you find these letters in the picture?

STORK

If I had known about my trail,
I'd never have become a snail.
It spells out everywhere I go,
No privacy at all, you know?

Can you find these letters in the picture?

SnAil

I love to eat the things I find,
In houses owned by humankind.
I'll raid your kitchen, make a din,
And spell disaster in your bin.

Can you find these letters that make the picture?

BABOON

Three letters make me — Did you know:
My antlers take a year to grow?
These are the biggest I've grown yet,
Next year, I'll grow a bigger set.

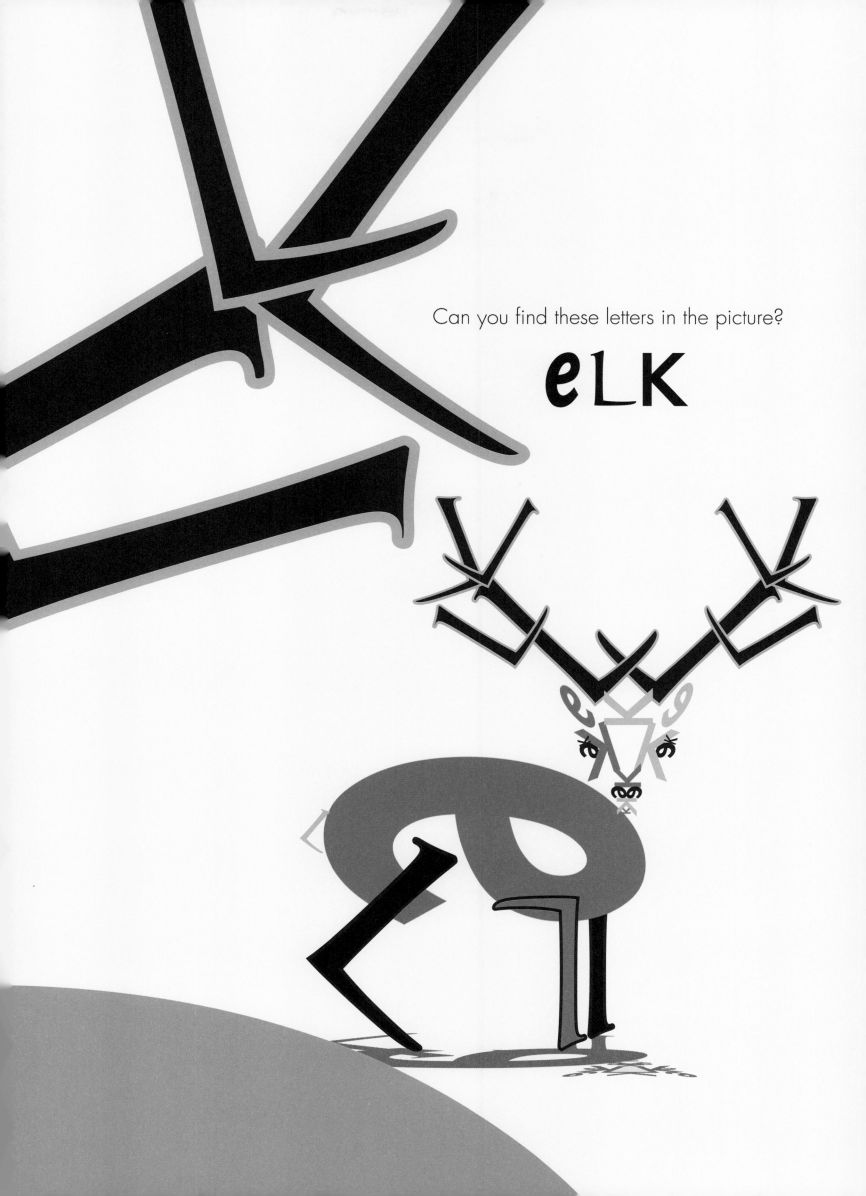

Can you find these letters in the picture?

eLK

Can you find these letters in the picture?

PELICAN

You'll notice when you spell this word,
The pelican's a hungry bird.
He scoops up breakfast, lunch and tea
With one swoop of that letter P.

You can do what toucans do
Twice as good as toucans, too.
Spell toucans, divide by one
Then multiply for twice the fun.

Can you find these letters in the picture?

TOUCAN

Despite such economic spelling,
Our rise to fame is quite compelling:
With so few letters; so few charms,
We made it to the coat-of-arms!

Can you find these letters that make the picture?

emu

I try to be the perfect Dad,
And babysit each kid we've had.
To each and every son and daughter,
I teach spelling, underwater.

SEAHORSE

Can you find these letters that make the picture?

Those of us born with red hair,
Like eating fruit in peace somewhere,
But, it's hard to hide in jungle scenes,
These orange letters, in those greens.

Can you find these letters in the picture?

oraNgUtaN

Thanks to the beauty of my spelling,
There is – you won't mind me retelling –
More style in my little feather,
Than all those chickens put together.

Can you find these letters that make the picture?

These letters make the picture. Can you find them all?

GRASSHOPPEr

I know I'm not a pretty face,
(I look like I'm from outer space),
But thighs like mine, spelled like machinery,
Jet-propel me through the scenery.

I hope you find my letters soon,
My skin is wrinkling like a prune.
I'm swimming 'round just getting wetter
While you look for every letter.

Can you find these letters in the picture?

GOLDfish

I really don't know where I'm at
When I can't find my habitat.
So spell me, and a tree to climb in?
(Bigger, please, than this one I'm in!)

Can you find these letters that make the picture?

KOALA

CLEVER KIDS TEACHERS' NOTES

ABOUT THIS BOOK & LETTER ART

Every picture in this book is made with the letters that spell its name. Each page has a 'letter key' which shows the exact letters and fonts that have been used to create each image. Find these letters in the image.

Look closely at the letters of the alphabet, and see if the shapes of the letters remind you of anything. If they do... that's the start of a Letter Art picture!

ABOUT TYPOGRAPHY

A A

A 'font' is a design for a set of letters of the alphabet. A serif font has letters with little 'feet'. A sans-serif font has letters without little 'feet'. Can you find examples of letters in these font styles in this book: **CAPITAL** lower case Sans-serif **Serif** Regular **Bold** *ITALIC* *Script*

ABOUT ANIMALS: Did you know...?

<u>Afghan Hounds</u> are an ancient breed whose long coats were ideal for the cold mountains of Afghanistan. Originally bred as hunting dogs, these 'sight hounds' are watchful and preoccupied, so they can often seem aloof.

<u>Armadillo.</u> The skin of the three-banded armadillo is made of thin, overlapping bone plates which form an 'armour' seal when it rolls up into a ball.

<u>Baboons</u> in South Africa have learned that it is more reliable, more rewarding and easier to raid houses for food than foraging for food in the wild.

<u>Beetles</u> constitute one quarter of all known animal life forms on earth, with around 400,000 species. In fact, the weight of the world's insect population (which is 10 quintillion in total or 1.4 billion insects to every person) is 70 times the weight of the human population.

<u>Budgerigars</u> can remember hundreds of words. One bird holds the world record, and is able to mimic over 1,700 words.

<u>Caterpillars</u> eat and eat and eat: they are the eating stage of the butterfly's life cycle. Butterflies eat very little — some species eat nothing at all. The full life cycle is: egg (3 to 4 days), caterpillar (about 2 weeks), chrysalis (10 to 14 days), and butterfly (2 days to 12 months).

<u>Chameleons</u> change their skin colour by rearranging the spaces between the crystals in their skin cells,which changes the way the cells reflect light and therefore changes the colour we see.

<u>Chimpanzees</u> share 98.8% of their DNA with humans, and are our closest living relatives. (Humans share 99.9% of the same DNA with all other humans, and only the last 0.1% is unique to each person.)

<u>Crabs</u> range from tiny Pea Crabs at just 4 mm (1/8 inch) wide, to the giant Japanese Spider Crab at up to 4 metres (13 feet) wide.

<u>Elk</u> antlers are made of bone. Elk grow new antlers every spring, and shed them every winter.

<u>Emu</u> fathers incubate the eggs and raise the chicks. The Emu features on the Australian national coat of arms, together with the kangaroo.

<u>Flamingos</u> become pinker the more crustaceans they eat, because the colour comes from the pink pigment in the crustacean shells.

<u>Frog.</u> The Red-Eyed Tree Frog has tiny suction cups on its toes to help it grip onto slippery surfaces in the moist rainforest.

<u>Goldfish</u> were originally silver. Breeders in ancient China took advantage of a genetic mutation to breed the popular orange or 'gold' varieties.

<u>Grasshoppers</u> can jump about a metre (just over 3 feet), which is 20 times their body length. They use a catapult mechanism to amplify the mechanical power of their muscles.

<u>Jellyfish</u> have existed for up to 700 million years, making them the oldest multi-organ animal group on earth.

<u>Koalas</u> are an endangered species, primarily because of habitat loss. Eucalypt trees provide both the koala's home and its food.

<u>Lion.</u> The male lion's mane protects his throat during territorial fights. The thicker the mane, the more chance the attacker's claws will get tangled there.

<u>Mandrill.</u> The world's largest monkey, the mandrill is the most colourful mammal of all. The colour is created by the way light is reflected from spaces between the fibres in the skin, and becomes even brighter if the animal is excited.

<u>Octopuses</u> have nine brains: one in the head, and one in each arm to control movement. They also have three hearts.

<u>Orangutans</u> are the gardeners of the rainforest. Eating fruit and spreading seeds as they wander, they regenerate the ecosystem for all jungle inhabitants.

<u>Ostrich.</u> The ostrich is the largest bird and fastest two-legged animal. It can run 72 mph (116 kph), while the cheetah runs 68 to 75 mph (110 to 120 kph), and the lion runs at 50 mph (80 kph).

<u>Owls</u> have long, tubular eyes shaped like telescopes. This means they can't look to the side, but must turn their whole head, and so they have adapted the ability to swivel their entire head up to 270 degrees.

<u>Peacock.</u> The Peafowl is native to India, but was soon adopted into the mythology of ancient Persians, Greeks and Romans. The male is called a peacock, and has feathers with an 'eyespot' design, to which humans throughout history have attributed great significance. The female is called a peahen.

<u>Pelicans</u> do not store their food in their bill, they use it as a fishing scoop. The bill can hold up to 3 gallons (11.35 litres) of water.

<u>Roosters</u> will prance or 'waltz', flapping their wings in a colourful display to let the other birds know they are healthy and strong.

<u>Seahorse.</u> The female deposits her eggs in the male's pouch, and he then carries up to 2,000 babies at a time for a period of 10 to 25 days.

<u>Snails</u> produce a slimy substance to keep their skin moist and to lubricate their path as they travel. This leaves a silver residue in their wake.

<u>Snakes</u> range from the tiny Threadsnake at 10 cm (4 inches) long, to the Anaconda at over 5 metres (16.5 feet) long, and 97 kg (214 lb) in weight.

<u>Squid</u> release ink into the water to conceal themselves from predators while they jet away. Some varieties make small ink clouds to serve as decoys.

<u>'Stallion'</u> refers to a male horse. Some other names for horse types are: mare, colt, filly, foal, hack, steed, mustang, bay, bronco, brumby, and cob.

<u>Storks</u> submerge their beaks underwater until they feel food. They snap their beaks shut in 25 milliseconds — the fastest reaction known in vertebrates.

<u>Swans</u> look so graceful because the head and neck stay still above water while their large feet paddle powerfully underwater. Swans also 'windsurf' across distances by holding up their wings like sails to take advantage of the breeze.

<u>Tigers</u> have striped skin, not just striped fur. Their stripes are like fingerprints and no two tigers have the same pattern.

<u>Toucans</u> are usually found in pairs. Their enormous beaks are extremely light-weight, made of a spongy material and bone struts.

<u>Whale.</u> A whale spout is not water, but air, exhaled through the whale's 'nose' or 'blowhole'. Any surrounding water is caught up in the burst upward.

DISCOVER MORE ABOUT LETTER ART, TYPOGRAPHY & OTHER RESOURCES AT:
www.melbournestyle.com.au or www.cleverkids.net.au